EFFECTIVE

MARKETING

IN THE DIGITAL AGE

How to Use Modern Marketing Methods to
Create and Maintain an Ongoing Conversation
With Your Customers & Community

Tim Dini

EFFECTIVE MARKETING IN THE DIGITAL AGE

Copyright © 2016 Tim Dini

For information contact:
www.timdini.com

Book and Cover design by Tim Dini

ISBN-13: 978-1535031707
ISBN-10: 1535031700

First Edition: July 2016

I want to say 'thank you' to everyone who helped make this book possible, especially my customers, without whom I would not have learned the real world lessons that made this information available, and to their customers who provided the experience and feedback that define effective marketing today.

"Businesses that fail to embrace modern marketing methods will soon be left behind; wondering what just happened."

- Tim Dini

Contents

CHAPTER ONE

Introduction: It Takes a Village

"The Internet is becoming the town square for the global village of tomorrow." - Bill Gates

Has this happened to you in the past couple of years? You come home from work and there on your doorstep is something you had forgotten even existed: The new Yellow Pages directory.

"Wow! There's still a Yellow Pages? Really?!"

Business owners during the first couple of decades of the 21st century understand that the way customers find products and services has been changing.

For most people, the Yellow Pages go right into the recycling bin because it is an archaic 20th century search tool in the digital age. It's much faster, easier and more efficient to get the information you need by using your smart phone, laptop or iPad. Not only can you get literally thousands of options in a split second, but you can view images, compare similar products and even review what other customers are saying.

This represents a sea-change in the way business owners should approach marketing. Buying newspaper ads is a waste of money when nobody is reading newspapers anymore. Even television advertising - formerly considered to be the most effective (and expensive) way to reach consumers - is waning in its ability to penetrate markets because of the new streaming video options many consumers prefer.

If the 21st century business owner hopes to succeed in this new market environment, then he or she needs to consider more creative, innovative and effective ways to reach customers. Businesses need to build a virtual village of online fans who are not only loyal customers but advocates of their products and services to others. And business owners need to link their villages to other villages created by other business owners so that both can benefit from each other's efforts.

In short, here in the opening decades of the 21st century, it takes a village to build a business.

Interactive Conversations

One of the first steps towards building that village is using interactive conversations.

Interactive what?

Interactive conversations are a business model based on building interpersonal one-on-one relationships with your customers.

In the pre-internet world, this usually meant starting up a conversation with someone who walks into your store:

"Nice weather we're having. Can I help you find something? I like your shoes!"

This type of relationship building puts your customer at ease, makes them feel like they are welcome and appreciated, and lets them know that you are ready, willing and able to serve them.

But how do we chat up our online customers?

If, for example, your business's web page gets 1,000 hits per day, how can you make sure each of the 1,000 people who navigated to your page get that same sense of familiarity and comfort that your 20th century customers received when they visited your brick and mortar store?

That's where interactive conversations come into play.

Interactive conversations are a rich media experience that gives customers who visit your web page the illusion that there's an actual person behind the screen speaking with them online.

These interactions have a tone that is unique to your company. It can be friendly, helpful, a little edgy, laid back, even funny. Whatever personality works best for your business.

Like the 20th century sales clerk who chatted up customers when they walked through your front door, the virtual host of an interactive conversation responds in real time to your customer's questions and needs, while maintaining the personality that you want to project.

Interactive conversations can ask simple, straight-forward questions and use the information gleaned from your customers' answers to put them into different categories, such as:

- Interested but just looking
- Ready to buy but looking for best value
- Ready to buy - wanting to complete transaction as quickly as possible
- Frequent, loyal customer

Or whatever categories you choose.

This kind of lead qualifying and scoring can improve the way your virtual host interacts with the customer so that they can give each customer precisely what they want as quickly and efficiently as possible.

Building Brick and Mortar Businesses in a Virtual World

Interactive conversation is not new. In fact, it's being used by companies all over the world and is even something that many customers have come to expect from businesses.

Have you called your cable company or your bank lately? You probably were directed to a program that asked you questions, then directed you to the information you needed based on your responses.

This type of phone tree is a bare-bones interactive conversation method.

For a more sophisticated example, we need to look no further than to one of the most popular apps today, 'Siri'.

Siri is a virtual assistant available on the iPhone that allows users to ask questions and even get recommendations from a friendly and helpful voice that lives in their smart phone.

Siri is basically an ongoing interactive conversation that efficiently connects her owner to whatever they are seeking in a manner that borders on affectionate and even playful. Have you ever seen someone when they are first introduced to Siri? Most people find her absolutely delightful and will spend hours asking her all kinds of silly questions to see how she will respond.

Siri is successful because she gives people something that they want:

A personalized experience that is both entertaining and effective. When these are provided, users are willing to temporarily suspend their knowledge that they are interacting with a voice-recognition program linked to a response algorithm that uses a search engine.

The success of Siri should serve as a model for modern businesses seeking unique and entertaining ways to interact with their customers. Delighting the customer while simultaneously directing them toward the products and services you want them to buy will always be a formula for success.

The Digital Age Customer

Have you ever found a business model that had you thinking ...

"Wow! We should be doing that!"

Maybe it was the first time you walked into a bank and all the employees looked up and gave you a warm friendly greeting (a model they borrowed from Japanese sushi bars, incidentally), or perhaps it was when you went into an Apple store and encountered the laid back, no pressure, almost slacker-like "geniuses" who patiently explained the features and benefits of each product.

Your customers have had the same experiences. Once they encounter an innovative, friendly, helpful and efficient way of getting the products and services they want, they are more likely to keep returning to that business even if it costs a little more.

The goal is to have that experience happen at your business.

Interactive conversations are a way of providing that kind of customer experience. So throw away your Yellow Pages and start building your marketing on models customers genuinely enjoy.

You need to invent your own type of Siri.

CHAPTER TWO

Engaging the Disengaged

"Almost overnight, the Internet's gone from a technical wonder to a business must." – Bill Schrader

We've all had bad customer service experiences. You don't have to treat a customer disrespectfully to get them to walk out your door unhappy (although that's probably the fastest way). It can be something as simple as not giving clear, sensible answers to their questions, giving them the hard sell when they aren't ready for it, or even failing to give them the attention they expect.

Ever been ignored while standing in line at the deli? Infuriating!

Interactive conversations can help prevent your customers from experiencing these types of issues because your program can be designed to give your customers exactly what they want by mining a lot of information from just a few simple questions.

For example, the question "What can I help you with today?" can tell you right away whether your visitor is just researching information or is ready to buy.

Customers who are 'just looking' can be led to product recommendations or places where they can get additional research useful for finding the information they need.

With interactive conversations, you can show your customer that you are listening to them and genuinely want to help them achieve their objective with as little hassle as possible.

Customers who are looking for a specific product and are ready to buy can be taken directly to what they are looking for and the transaction can be completed as quickly as possible. You also can take the opportunity to try to up-sell your customers by recommending other products they might like.

Amazon is a genius at this: Whenever you click to purchase a product on their site, a list automatically pops up of "*People Who Bought This Product Also Bought …*"

Effective interactive conversations create the illusion for your customers that there is someone on the other end who genuinely cares about helping them meet their goals. This is done by modeling human conversation so that the user feels appreciated and that the responder wants to help them.

You may be asking: Why not just get somebody to sit in front of a computer screen in the backroom of your business and let them live chat online with your customers? Two reasons:

Hopefully, your business will have enough volume to make this option financially impractical. And once your interactive conversation programs are set up, you don't have to pay them a salary.

Even the nicest of human beings have their bad days and are prone to say things they regret later. Interactive conversations programs never have bad days and will always treat your customers exactly the way you want them to.

When your customers visit your site and are assisted by a caring, helpful virtual host who is committed to getting them what they want while at the same time nurturing an interpersonal relationship with them, your customers are going to be impressed and will want to do business with you again and again.

Converting Visitors into Customers

As a business owner, you can differentiate your customer's service experience at your business by making it unique, enjoyable and memorable.

Look at the *Trader Joe's* grocery chain. Laid back grocery clerks in Hawaiian shirts helpfully guide customers to the natural, quirky and slightly exotic products they want. Before you know it, you're walking out of TJ's with several shopping bags full of food you never even knew existed. *Black bean and quinoa infused tortilla chips? Who knew?*

This same type of experience creation can be attained with interactive conversations.

Once you guide your customers to your web page using the same avenues you probably already use like ...

- Paid Search
- Display Ads
- Banner Ads
- SMS Text Messages
- Outbound Email Campaigns
- Television Commercials
- Radio Spots
- Direct Mail

... you can immerse them in a fun, lively and helpful experience that will make them want to return to your website again and again.

A series of brief questions can quickly help you identify why each individual customer has landed on your page. This information is important to know in order to create a pleasant interactive experience for your visitors.

To get maximum value from their responses, it's important to follow simple guidelines. Here are some valuable points to keep in mind when developing your interactive conversations:

Eight Interactive Conversation Guidelines

1. Keep it Simple: Only give visitor's one task to accomplish at a time.

2. Yes/No/Maybe: Provide only a limited number of possible responses.

3. Keep it Relevant: Give your visitors only meaningful choices.

4. Avoid Confusion: Make it clear to your visitors what they should do at every moment.

5. Eliminate Distractions: Keep their attention focused on the task at hand.

6. Don't Challenge Them: Make answering your questions as easy as possible.

7. Keep Them Aware: If you are waiting for them to respond, make sure they know you are waiting.

8. Keep it Moving: If they don't respond in a timely fashion, pause, quit or move on to something else.

Gathering data about what your customers want is vitally important to being able to provide it to them. As you do so, you can improve the chances of your customer returning to your site by creating an effective brand.

The Quaker Oats Story: Building Brand Loyalty

What comes to mind when you think of *Quaker Oats*. Probably a smiling guy in a pilgrim hat on the oatmeal box, right?

But you probably also have an emotional bond with the brand because it provides nutritious, delicious and affordable foods that you have been enjoying since you were a kid.

That's no accident.

Quaker Oats has mastered the skill of creating effective branding that effectively provokes emotional connections with its customers. You never would have guessed that the company associated closely with wholesome, healthful comfort foods is owned by *Pepsico*, the same company that at one time owned *Stolichnaya* vodka and *Kentucky Fried Chicken*, and markets the *Taco Bell* taco that uses *Doritos* for its shell.

Like any great brand, the fact that Quaker Oats brought those images and feelings to mind was intentional. In fact, there is an entire office building in downtown Chicago that is filled with people who spend their careers trying to discover ways to get you to associate good feelings with their products.

Your business may not have the deep pockets of Pepsico or Quaker Oats, but your interactive conversation program can still assist you in creating a powerful brand around you and your products and services.

Even with a small budget, you can still build brand loyalty around your products and services in four highly effective ways:

1. Creating a Unique and Friendly Tone

Let's return for a moment to Siri. There's no question that most iPhone users love her (or is she an, it?) Apple purposely designed the app so that it is both helpful and playful, even a little coy, which users find intriguing.

2. Providing Consistently High-Quality, High-Value Interactions

Visitors to your site should take something valuable away from it, even if they don't buy anything. This could include recommendations for additional research, a comparison of prices for the same products from your chief competitors, or anything else that sends the message that you genuinely want to help them.

3. Good Reputation

You've probably seen the market research: A person who has a positive experience with your business may tell one or two other people, but someone who has had a negative experience will tell 10 people or more. Building and maintaining the good reputation of your business, is one of the most important goals of any successful marketing effort. Interactive conversations can help both standardize customer interactions to prevent negative experiences and personalize them so that customers feel welcome and appreciated.

4. Build Personal Relationships

Despite the fact that interactive conversations are pre-designed programs, it is possible to get your visitors to suspend their disbelief and actually believe that they are interacting with a warm, caring human being. Combined with other techniques which we will discuss shortly, this can be the single biggest technique for converting customers into loyal followers and raving fans of your business.

The purpose of interactive conversations is therefore twofold. Obviously, you want your customers to buy what you are selling and to make it as easy as possible to do so. But the second purpose is to create loyalty bonds with your customers that build an effective brand that your customers associate with positive feelings.

Grabbing Your Customers Attention and Demanding a Response

So by now you're probably asking:

How can a pre-designed program build the illusion that visitors to your website are interacting with an actual human being

*who cares about what they want and is devoted to helping
them in any way they can?*

Glad you asked, because this is the core of interactive conversations.

An interactive conversations program in its simplest form is a response tree that directs visitors to various forks based on their actions. Notice that we said *actions* not *answers.*

That's because sometimes your visitors' inactions can tell you as much about what they want as their answers to your questions.

An effective interactive conversation will specifically respond with human intelligence and even emotion to:

1. The Visitor's Actions

How they answer questions, what types of things within the site they click on or even how long they spend on a particular page within your site.

2. The User's Inactions

Including what questions they choose to ignore, and what pages they don't click on.

3. The User's Past Actions

Their search history, how many times they have visited your site in the past, how long they have spent on your site per visit.

4. A Series of the User's Actions

The sequence with which they navigate from page to page or from product to product within your site can provide valuable information which the interactive conversation program can use to make suggestions or offer help.

5. The Actual Time and Space That the User is in

Customers from various geographic locations may have particular product preferences, as will the time of day visitors are accessing your web page (in other words, 9 a.m. on a Monday vs. 2 a.m. on a Saturday).

The Comparison of Different Users' Situations and Actions

Comparing the action of one particular visitor to your site with the similar actions of previous visitors can help you predict the expected outcome.

The data collected by your interactive conversations program can then be used to create a high-value experience for your visitors with the intention of converting them into both short and long-term customers. To accomplish this goal, the program provides responses designed to build personal relationships with your visitors.

This can be done by:

1. Using Dialogue That Conveys a Sense of Intimacy

Using first names, referencing personal details and preferences, empathizing with the visitor's problems.

2. Maintaining Professionalism

Balancing familiarity with responses that are appropriate and proper, using humor when possible but avoiding sarcasm.

3. Avoiding Repetition

Providing identical responses breaks down the wall of suspended belief, reminding visitors that they are interacting with a program. A better plan is to provide a variety of similar but not identical responses so that the fantasy is maintained.

4. Acknowledge the Visitor's Gender

Creating responses that are gender-specific is one of the fastest and easiest ways to defeat the one-size-fits-all prejudice against automated programs. Subtle yet effective techniques such as these can be used to better tailor your interaction with specific customer sets.

5. Provide a Seamless Experience

Anything that gets between your customers reaching his or her objective while on your site needs to be removed. This will sustain the customer's belief that they are dealing with an actual caring person and guide them more efficiently to the desired outcome.

When your interactive conversations program is designed with these guidelines in mind, you can create a customer service experience that is both memorable and rewarding, will keep them returning to your site again and again, and will convert them into raving fans who will recommend your business to their friends and acquaintances.

RoboFixer: Continually Improving Efficiencies

It's no coincidence that a recurring theme in many science fiction stories and movies are machines that become so intelligent that humans become obsolete.

It's an inherent fear of human beings that putting so much trust in a mechanical machine or digital program will ultimately result in our own destruction.

But that's all just science fiction, right? Right?!

So far, humanity is safe from destruction by evil robots because advances in artificial intelligence have yet to overcome the imagination and creativity of the human mind.

Still, it is possible to design your interactive conversation program so that it can become smarter as it goes along. And its analytics are critical for providing you with the data you need to make the most effective decisions for your business.

On a global level, interactive conversation programs can collect data on user responses, completion rates, time spent per question, and other information; then automatically compile this data to continually optimize the conversation to improve performance.

On an individual level, the program can keep track of your customers' personal preferences and interests. It can then use this information to solidify the interpersonal relationship between the customer and your business.

A very simple example would be collecting birthday information then sending an e-card or special offer to customers a few days before their birthday.

Or, it can be as sophisticated as the tool used by the digital video recorder service; TiVo, or online video streaming services such as NetFlix, which make recommendations of programming users might enjoy based on their previous viewing habits.

CHAPTER THREE

140 Characters or Less

"Our printing press is the Internet. Our coffee houses are social networks." - Heather Brooke

Business owners planning their marketing in this second decade of the 21st century face challenges that were unimaginable only a decade ago.

In addition to the age old problems of increased marketing expenses and always needing more customers, today's businesses now must struggle with building and maintaining a vast social media network, competing with other businesses that have crafted more effective social media networks, and counteracting negative customer reviews posted to aggregate review sites.

These types of issues are the downside of the universal internet access that was created by huge advances in data storage technology and the subsequent plummeting of the costs. Nearly everyone is now online and is now discovering the free tools available to make their voices heard.

For the business owner who is able to manage his or her marketing program through these changes, the rewards are abundant:

Increased customer satisfaction and referrals, a better understanding of what their customers actually want, a heightened community profile, and even lower operating expenses. All of which result in more revenues and the ability to sleep better.

The ability to master an effective social media campaign – such as being able to get your message across using only 140 characters, the maximum size of a single Tweet – requires a different skill set than simply buying newspaper advertisements or scripting a TV commercial. The sheer volume of content on the internet and the user's ability to filter that content to weed out spam requires successful internet marketers to make a personal connection.

In much the same way that an interactive conversation program can delight your website visitors while seeking relevant information, your internet marketing program needs to provide your customers with enough high-value content that they keep opening your emails and visiting your web pages.

Before we begin an examination of how to do that, it perhaps will be helpful to review how we got to this place and what it means for your business.

Six Causes of the Emergence of Social Media

In 1970, the most powerful computer in the world took up a room the size of a two-car garage and was operated by a technician feeding it a stack of punch cards, each of which carried a single instructional code.

Today, a slender Apple notebook has a billion times more storage capability, has a processor that works millions of times faster, and it can be used to stream high-definition video, download music and even play interactive games with people on the other side of the planet.

You might say the technology has improved a little in the past 40 years.

When the internet first started to gain widespread use, it was primarily a tool for conducting academic research, but once users began to realize how easy it could be used to communicate with other people, especially those who shared common interests, social media emerged as one of the primary uses of the internet.

When the people began abandoning traditional forms of media in favor of the web, businesses desperate to survive soon followed. This was beneficial to both consumers and businesses because:

1. Scope: Unlike traditional media, social media has the ability to reach millions of people instantly.

2. Target Ability: Unlike traditional media, which distributes a broad message in the hopes that it will be seen by the small percentage of interested customers, social media can be directed at highly-targeted customers

who already have shown a proven interest in your products.

3. Accessibility: While traditional media is available only to those with the substantial capital expenditure to afford it, social media can be used by anybody at little or no cost.

4. Usability: Technical skill and advanced training are not a prerequisite for creating and maintaining social media. In fact, most platforms come complete with free tools that make it easy to upload content, images, video, audio files, slide shows, and even live webinars.

5. Instantaneousness: There's no production downtime with social media. If you think it, you can post it, Tweet it or otherwise broadcast it in a matter of seconds.

6. Edit Ability: Social media gives marketers the ability to quickly replace, modify or remove any message instantly. Or you can supplement your postings with comments.

Perhaps the biggest difference between social media marketing and traditional marketing is that social media allows users to interact as part of a community, rather than just being a targeted end user.

Instead of simply reading a print ad or watching a television commercial, your customers can respond, react, enhance, share and even promote your marketing as a contributing member of the community that your marketing created.

When you create a social media marketing campaign, you are really creating an entire culture, a kind of community in which your customers can participate as active members.

By continually providing high-value content to your customers without constantly trying to sell them something, you can populate that village with dedicated fans of your business who are passionately devoted to what you have to offer.

Your Social Media Campaign: Castles Made of Sand

Earlier we discussed how interactive conversations programs can capture your site visitors' imaginations so that they suspend their disbelief and willingly believe that they are talking to a real person, even if it is just a pre-designed program.

Your social media marketing program lets you take that even a step farther: You can create an entire universe in which your customers will willfully and gladly inhabit.

This is accomplished by building an online community of people with shared common interests, then offering everybody who joins your community something extremely valuable: a sense of belonging, loyalty and rewards.

What you are building are essentially fan clubs for your products, then incentivizing customers to join these fan clubs by offering them high-value content, exclusive access to insider information, and the feeling that they are an important part of the community you have created.

A lot of attention has been paid to the success of sites such as Groupon.com, which offer members deep discounts on local businesses products and services.

But these types of sites only offer half measures.

There are not very many customers who are fiercely loyal to Groupon and who look forward to getting their emails so they can learn more about what's going on over at company headquarters. *Groupon offers online coupons. That's basically it.*

What we're talking about is something much, much more. Offer your customers a Buy-One-Get-One Free (BOGO) offer and they might use it if it is for something they already wanted.

But what if you provided free high-value content related to your core niche that customers could actually use to improve their lives?

What if you encouraged your employees to post personal details about their lives, such as pictures of their kids and vacation videos?

What if you asked your customers for their opinions about operational issues and even conducted polls to determine, for example, where your next store should open or what sort of sale you should offer next month?

That would be a little different, wouldn't it? This is also innovative because these types of actions engage your customers in an ongoing conversation with your business.

When your customers feel they have been given special access to your business, when they feel like their opinion not only counts but can actually influence how your business operates, when they have an emotional bond to the people that work there, then they are likely to become fiercely loyal, raving fans of your business.

Unlike traditional media marketing, social media marketing offers you the tools to reach millions of people instantly, target exactly those customers you want most, create free and unlimited access to your community so your customers can jump in and out as much as they please, and modify anything that isn't working at a moment's notice.

Facebook and Its Discontents

In many ways, Facebook is a victim of its own success. It has become such an important part of so many people's lives that its users sometimes resent it.

That could explain why so many people looked on with glee when its Initial Product Offering (IPO) stumbled out of the gate in early 2012 and the outrage that erupted after it made the default email address of its members their Facebook email addresses.

Still, the site's influence is so pervasive that it's hard to imagine that Facebook has only been around since 2005.

The essential appeal of Facebook is that it allows people to feel that there is a community that revolves around their life. When somebody opens a Facebook account, creates a set of "Friends", posts comments, pictures, videos, and links to other pages, what they are really doing is celebrating themselves and asking other people to celebrate them as well.

It's funny how the character of self that we create on Facebook is always some sort of idealized version of ourselves: One who keeps in touch with friends from high school and college; swaps gossip with former co-workers; posts pictures of our pets, children and vacations; and shows our commitment to causes and beliefs by painlessly posting links on our home page.

That's because Facebook simultaneously gives us exposure and anonymity.

It's like wearing a mask to a costume ball, which allows us to behave any way we like but without ever really exposing our true feelings to the ball's other masked guests.

Many businesses have Facebook pages but don't really know what to do with them.

Occasionally, they will post a status update advertising specific products or upcoming promotions, but they don't make an effort to engage their followers. And that's too bad because if people care enough about your business to join your Facebook page, it's a good bet they are pretty passionate about your products and services.

Facebook offers your business this same opportunity to craft whatever image you want for it. When you create a Facebook fan page, you get to decide what goes on it and what doesn't.

Things to Include: Pictures from the company picnic and holiday party, celebratory profiles of your top employees, information about upcoming events.

Things to Leave Off: Anything that doesn't celebrate your company.

Maintaining an effective Facebook marketing plan requires a lot of work, but it offers a lot of payoff because of the way people are linked to each other on the site. When somebody leaves a comment on your Facebook fan page, a link to that comment shows up on each of their friends' Facebook pages as well.

Once you have created your Facebook fan page, you need to promote it so that people can find it. It goes without saying that you should include links to your company's Facebook fan page anywhere you possibly can, including emails, mailings, invoices, web pages, blogs, etc. - but that alone won't be enough to create the community you need to build your business. You are going to have to actively recruit Friends.

Fortunately, doing this is relatively easy. The first places you want to visit are any fan pages or forums on Facebook that are devoted to your company's product niche.

If you own a car dealership that specializes in European sports cars, then there are fan pages devoted to enthusiasts of that niche.

If you sell financial services, there are pages dedicated to observing and commenting upon changes in the markets.

You should not limit yourself just to Facebook either. The big search engines - Google, Yahoo and Bing - host forums on nearly every topic imaginable. And there are millions of bloggers writing about different topics as well.

Once you have identified where the people who are interested in your niche are located, the next step is to establish your reputation on these sites:

DON'T - Post ads, push the hard sell, or come off in any way as a self-promoter or grandstander.

No one visits fan pages or posts of blogs looking for commercials. If you annoy other forum members with these kinds of antics, you will be harming, rather than helping, your reputation.

DO - Be a friendly, helpful and active participant. Offer free high-value content, such as links to websites with information relevant to your product niche or articles on interesting niche-related topics. Provide lots of personal information, personal history, private photos, and other content that basically will make your life an open book for others to peruse at their pleasure.

Treat other forum members the way you would treat an old, trusted friend. This will help your prospective customers create an emotional bond with you, opening the door to interpersonal relationships.

And always, always, always include a link to your business's fan page and invite people to "Like" it. This will create a link on their home page to your fan page and lets you automatically share any new content with them whenever you post it.

But don't stop there.

Besides creating and maintaining your business's fan page, create another fan page devoted to your product niche but not branded with your company's brand. Add some high-value content to it that is niche-related, not business-related. Then join the ten most popular other fan pages in that niche and send an invitation to your niche fan page to each of their members.

Keep your members engaged by constantly replying to their forum posts, offering praise and trying to learn more about their personal interests. After you have populated your niche-related fan page with a good number of people with a shared interest, you can then slowly begin to introduce recommendations and reviews for your own products and services.

Facebook may be momentarily down, but it's not out. The fact that it has more than 700 million members means that it's likely to remain an influential and effective way to reach millions of people instantly and for free.

As an effective 21st century business marketer, you simply need to make sure you are using it to maintain a lively and never-ending conversation with your prospective customers.

Excuse Me, Did You Just Tweet?

Facebook is a gateway drug to Twitter. Once you get hooked on Twitter, it's really hard to get off of it.

The appeal to Twitter is its brevity. With only 140 characters to work with, Twitter users have no choice but to be direct and to the point. That allows users to very quickly scroll through hundreds of Tweets in only a few minutes.

Most people use Twitter as a way to keep up with friends, family and people you know, but you can get a glimpse of the lives of people you don't know, including your favorite celebrities and sports stars.

For internet savvy 21st century business marketers, Twitter also is increasingly becoming a highly effective marketing tool.

With Twitter, you can post links to pictures, videos and documents. That makes it a highly effective way to get your products and services in front of a lot of people instantly and for free.

Because people can be linked instantly with a big group of people both who they know and who they don't know, and can access that community from their smart phone, laptop, PC, iPad or even from their television set, Twitter has become one of the most immediate and tangible forms of communication ever created.

To save you time and to get twice the value from your work, you want to link your Twitter to your Facebook and vice-versa. That way, each time you post on one site it automatically will post on the other. It's easy to do; just follow the instructions on either site. Also, promote your Twitter feed everywhere you promote your Facebook page.

Since the goal with Twitter is to get the highest number of followers, when you are first starting out, search for people you know, including loyal customers, family, friends, acquaintances, co-workers, and current and former school mates. Use the search function to look for their names then follow them.

Next, go to their profile and see who they are following. You can follow all of these people if you want, but a better way would be to look for people you either know or friends of friends and follow them.

The next thing you want to do is to search for terms related to your business niche. This is done by performing a search using a hash tag (#).

If, for example, you are in the pest control business, search for #PestControl and all the tweets from people who included the hash tag #PestControl will appear. Many of these are potential customers, so you will want to follow these people.

Whenever you follow somebody, they get a notification that you are following them. In most cases, people will be polite and will follow you back. As they do, your list of Twitter followers will begin to grow with people who are passionate about the niche.

Now that you have some followers, here are some tips to help you build your list of Twitter followers quickly:

1. Promote Your Twitter Profile Everywhere: Always include a link to your Twitter profile on your other social media sites, on your blogs, any articles you write, on your web page and anywhere else you can. The easier you can make it for people to find you on Twitter, the more followers you can accumulate.

2. Follow Your Followers: Whenever anybody follows you, make sure you reciprocate. This helps build a bond between you and it also lets you see what they are Tweeting.

3. Respond to People When They Tweet You: Twitter notifies you anytime your Twitter address is mentioned in another Tweet, even if it was not directed at you. Always follow up with the sender. Remember: Your goal is to make your followers your friend first. Once you accomplish this, they will be more likely to become loyal customers. Also, always respond to direct messages in order to build your customer base.

4. Be Funny and Informative: Because most people follow hundreds of people, they usually just scroll through dozens of Tweets until they find something they like. If your tweets are funny and informative, they will always look forward to them so they will stop to read them. Don't just post links to products. If you do, it's unlikely your followers will ever stop to look at your Tweets. Instead, engage your followers one-on-one and find ways to build relationships with them.

5. Tweet & Retweet: Twitter lets you forward anyone's Tweet with the click of a single button. When you find something interesting, share it with your followers. And when your followers Tweet something relevant, retweet it.

6. Participate in Group Discussions: You can look for Tweets about topics that interest you by doing a search using a hash tag. For example, if your business is in sports memorabilia, you can find every Tweet in which that niche was tagged by searching #sportsmemorabilia.

7. Use Lists to Organize Followers: Twitter makes it easy to arrange your followers according to specific parameters. When you organize your followers into groups, you can more easily target specific Tweets at specific groups.

8. Say What You Think, Not Just What You Are Doing: Unlike Facebook, where users like to see what their Friends are doing, Twitter users usually prefer to know what the people they are following are actually thinking. This is a great way to promote your business because you can give positive mini-reviews and then provide the link

for your followers to purchase the items from your website.

9. Don't Start a Tweet With @: Remember: The @ symbol is the first character in a Twitter user's address, so if you send a Tweet to @FlorenceAndTheMachine, for example, only she will get that Tweet.

To supercharge Twitter as a marketing tool, you want a huge list of people with an interest in the types of product or services you are marketing.

To do this, search for tweets about your niche. Say, for example, you are selling products related to the horseracing industry. Simply conduct a search for "#horseracing".

Then go to the profiles of people who have recently tweeted in this niche and look at their list of followers. If they have a lot of followers, follow those people. In most cases, they will automatically follow you back. When they do, every time you tweet something, they will receive it and there is the possibility they will retweet it so that their followers will see it as well.

Next go through their list of followers and look for those people with the highest number of followers. These are the people you want to follow to build your marketing program because they offer a point of contact to the most people.

Twitter is an excellent marketing tool because once you build a long list of followers, you can reach all of them instantly simply by sending a tweet. Build your list of followers with people who are interested in the niche your product is in, then set about the task of building relationships with your followers.

You want to build relationships with your followers, not try to sell them something all the time. Instead, send Tweets that are about your niche but are not related to specific products. One good way to do this is to use Google or Bing to find articles about your niche, then copy and paste interesting facts about your niche subject and send them out as tweets:

"Here's 10 Top Handicapping Tips for Your Next Trip to the Track: http://www.winningponies.com/help/10-basic-handicapping-tips.html/ #horseracing"

Another effective technique is to find jokes and sayings about your niche subject. Everybody loves humor, so just search jokes about your niche then copy and paste them and send them out as tweets.

You can do the same thing with sayings about your niche:

"A horse gallops with his lungs, Perseveres with his heart, and wins with his character. - Tesio #horseracing"

"Horse sense is the thing a horse has which keeps it from betting on people. - W C Fields #horseracing"

"There is no secret so close as that between a rider and his horse. - R S Surtees from Mr. Sponge's Sporting Tour #horseracing"

You don't have to stick to your niche, either. Tweet about anything you want, as long as it is upbeat and positive. If you are not always cheerful and friendly, your followers won't want to stop and read your tweets as they scroll through the thousands they receive each day.

You want to connect with your followers on a personal level, so reveal things about your personal life in your tweets. Once you become a trusted friend of your followers, it will be easier to convince them to buy the products you are promoting once you begin promoting them.

A good rule of thumb is to limit your promotion tweets to three times per week. Any more than that and your followers might think you are spamming them and may un-follow you.

Spend the rest of the time building bonds with your followers by sending non-promotional tweets both about your niche subject and unrelated to your niche subject, emphasizing your personal life.

When one of your followers sends out an interesting tweet, retweet it so that the rest of your followers can read it too. The person who originally send it out will get a notification that you retweeted their tweet, and that will improve your standing in their eyes.

But don't automatically retweet every tweet you get or you will be seen as a spammer. Instead, retweet the best tweets from your followers. Tack on a personal message and it will help build relationships with your followers.

Finally, trending topics are those topics that are most popular at any given moment. They will appear on your main Twitter page. Keeping an eye on trending topics is helpful to the Twitter marketer because you can see what people are tweeting about right now.

If your niche subject is trending, it is a good time to start getting your message out because more people will see it.

Why Google is the 500-Pound Gorilla of the Future

Google+ was supposed to be Google's answer to Facebook. It was a rival designed to offer many of the same functions and improve on others. Because Facebook pretty much invented social media and has dominated the industry for so long, Google was slow to grow among users and never got near the popularity of Facebook. But while recent articles pronouncing Google+ as dead may show evidence of its demise, Google has responded by creating Google My Business, something business owners need to embrace, and quickly.

Google My Business offers something Facebook pages cannot: The benefit of being able to integrate the power of its massive search engine into social networking. For example, when a user wants to find a particular business page, they only have to add the "+" symbol in front of their search term to be taken directly to that page. This is especially helpful for businesses that rely on a lot of searches because it can speed things up dramatically.

Another advantage Google My Business has over Facebook pages is that the site is integrated into its other popular products, such as Gmail, YouTube, Chrome and Android, setting the stage for Google to promote branded business pages simultaneously, something that Twitter and Facebook can't do, at least not yet.

There are a lot of businesses who opt for Facebook and Twitter as their primary social media platforms, relegating Google to the margins, but Google My Business offers a lot of benefits that Facebook and Twitter can't.

Despite Facebook's raising about $100 billion in its IPO in early 2012, Google is the bigger gorilla in the internet jungle. Through its research and development and its acquisitions, Google has positioned itself as the biggest player in the industry for many years to come.

The fact that Google+ didn't take off right out of the gate means nothing. The new Google My Business page actually offers users more options than Facebook, Twitter, YouTube, LinkedIn and all the other social media platforms combined.

For example, Google not only allows you to share your status updates and photos, but they can be shared on the much larger Google platform, across all of Google's online properties. It also allows video chat using Hangouts. In a relatively short period of time, Google My Business may evolve into becoming a massively interconnected digital community that businesses will feel compelled to take advantage of, if not outright forced to.

CHAPTER FOUR

Do You Remember Rock & Roll Radio?

"Information design has been around since the 1970's ... But now with the rise of the Internet, it's having something of a second birth." – David McCandless

You may be familiar with the Ramones song from the 1980s that was called "Do You Remember Rock and Roll Radio?" It's an amazing song that celebrated a bygone era of 1950s rock and roll, all backed up by a driving Phil Spector "Wall of Sound" production.

The song is so joyous that it practically defies you not to tap your feet and sing along with the chorus.

That's the type of community you want to create with your business's marketing program: Infectious, lively and irresistible.

Like the Ramones classic hit, the interactive conversations on your web pages, your Facebook and Twitter posts, and every other aspect of your marketing program should practically defy your customers not to have fun and join in the celebration. You want to invite your customers to join the party, have fun and enjoy themselves. If you can create this type of atmosphere, customers will flock to your business.

For example, think back a couple of years ago when Apple first introduced the iPod. It produced a series of commercials which featured a set of quick cuts of black silhouettes of young people against day-glow colors dancing to such songs as Daft Punk's "Technologic", the Black Eyed Peas' "Hey Mama" and the Jet's "Are You Gonna Be My Girl?"

Any time one of those ads came on TV, people couldn't help but to watch them. Not only were they bright, bouncy and fun to watch, but they evoked a spirit of youthful energy backed by driving, cutting-edge-yet-approachable music. In short, they were cool. And they made everyone say, "Man, I have got to get one of those iPods!"

Your business may not be selling cool digital music devices like iPods, but you can still create the same kind of fun and inviting marketing that will make people want to be part of the party no matter what you sell.

One good way to start thinking about how to do this is by brainstorming ideas. Start with the phrase, "You know what would be really cool? ..." and finish the phrase with a marketing idea for your business. Repeat this process over and over until you have a sizeable list of great ideas. Don't limit yourself to the practical: Think large! You will be surprised by how creative you can be.

In this section, we are going to take a look at some of the other types of online marketing platforms you can use to build fun, lively and irresistible marketing plans.

What I Really Want to Do Is Direct: Why Everybody Should Be Video Marketing

My, how times have changed. It wasn't all that long ago that if you wanted to make your own films, it required a Super 8 camera, reels and reels of film, and a rack of bright lights. And even then, the quality probably wasn't very good, plus you needed a film projector to show it.

A couple of years later, the VHS camera came out. It was certainly easier to use than a film camera, but at more than $1,000 each, they were prohibitively expensive for most people.

Today, advances in data storage have allowed electronics manufacturers to put a video camera on just about every device – your laptop, smart phone, even your iPod. Even high definition video cameras can be purchased for less than two hundred dollars, and they are about the size of a pack of baseball cards. But the quality they provide is intense.

Because everybody now has video cameras, watching video has become the method of choice for internet users. Why bother reading through blocks of boring text when you can simply watch fun, colorful and entertaining videos? Anybody can make them, they are free to post and if they are cool and interesting, you can get millions of people to watch them.

Plus we're only at the beginning of the video age, sort of like 100 years ago we were only at the beginning of the automobile age. Don't be one of the *(soon-to-be-out-of)* business owners thinking online video marketing is a fad. You can almost imagine the owner of a horse and carriage shop telling his employees ...

"Don't worry, these things will never catch on."

You can drive a lot of traffic to your pages with an effective video marketing campaign and it no longer requires a lot of expensive equipment or technical expertise. If you have any device with a built-in video camera, play around with it for a little while until you can figure out how to get the best quality video you can.

If you have a digital camera, for example, use your tripod if you have one to stabilize the image. If you don't own a tripod and are planning to create a lot of videos to promote your products then you may want to consider investing in a tripod. You can find a bare bones one that will suit your needs quite well for just a few dollars. Or bid on one on eBay.

If you aren't sure you will be shooting a lot of video and don't want to invest anything yet, at least set the camera on a flat surface so that your video isn't shaky. A lot of cameras today even come with built-in digital image stabilizers, so yours may already have one.

There are a number of different kinds of videos. Take a few minutes to research videos about products like the ones you are promoting and see what your competitors are doing. What do they do that you like? Model that idea. What don't you like? Avoid that idea.

One common type of video is just to record someone talking about your product. It could be you, a friend or just about anybody. Try shooting a video showing how your product works, or what services your company provides. Explain what its benefits are, and how it will improve the lives of the people who buy it.

Keep the video short, less than 2 or 3 minutes. Keep your video lively and entertaining, but always promise to reveal more and more information as you go on so your viewers will keep watching all the way through.

Because you are familiar with your product's benefits and how to sell them, you don't necessarily have to write a script, but you will probably want to map out some talking points at the very least. If you are using the camera on your computer, you can put your script or talking points on the screen to make it easier to remember what you want to say.

If you are just shooting yourself talking about the product, the video should have this kind of structure:

- Greet your viewers and introduce yourself
- Introduce your product
- Talk a little about the product's benefits
- If you can demonstrate how it works, do so
- Near the end, reveal something special about the product

Conclude with the Call to Action: Tell your viewers exactly what it is you want them to do, such as visit your website or explain how they can buy your product.

If you are not used to being on camera, try to relax as much as possible. Remember to be friendly and helpful. One helpful tip is to talk with your hands more than you normally would. This helps creates inflection in your voice and is more interesting to listen to than just a monotone.

The second kind of video is a series of static screen shots, such as a PowerPoint presentation. They can actually be created with PowerPoint, if you already have the program, or you can download a program that will allow you to build one. You can download any number of free software programs that you can use to get started.

These kinds of videos are going to be more like commercials than testimonials or sales pitches. You definitely are going to want it scripted. If you are not confident about your script writing abilities, there are many experienced writers on eLance.com, Guru.com or even Fiverr.com who would be happy to create a script for you for very little money.

But if you want to give it a try yourself, the script should be set up so that there is one line for each slide. The lines should be very short, usually not more than ten words, which means you will have to be very economical with your writing. And obviously, the line should be relevant to what is displayed on the screen.

Studies show that the human mind can processes images and audible impressions much faster than most people would believe.

Each slide will be on the screen only for about 3 seconds, no more than 5, except for the last slide which will stay onscreen until it fades out. That means for a 2 minute video, you are going to need about 25 to 35 lines of text.

When you type out your script, it should look like this:

Buddy Baker Racing School
Total Lines: 15
Total Running Time (approx. minutes): 1:00:00

Buddy Baker Racing School Video Script:

"Have you always dreamed of driving a race car?"

"Screaming around a race track at top speeds?"

"Driving a race car is an experience you'll never forget."

"But where can you learn to drive a race car safely?"

"The Buddy Baker Racing School teaches the skills that professionals use on the track. You'll learn what it takes to be competitive in stock car racing, with state-of-the-art equipment!"

Your videos don't always have to be about your products, either. Some of the most popular types of videos are those that show people how to do something.

You can create "how to" videos that are related to your product, or you can simply create videos that explains how to do something that is your hobby or that you are good at.

You can post these videos on your pages to build relationships with your customers, you can give them away as a free download on your squeeze page (more on that in a moment), or you can post them on video sharing sites. Make sure you include tags that are related to what your video is about so that people can find them.

Here are some of the most popular video sharing sites:

- YouTube.com
- Vimeo.com
- Screen.Yahoo.com
- DailyMotion.com
- LiveLeak.com
- Vine.co
- Ustream.tv
- Break.com

- MySpace.com (yes, it's still there and slowly getting popular again)
- Metacafe.com
- Veoh.com

Distributing your video is very easy, but you'll need to create an account with each individual video site before you can upload your videos, or you can simply sign up for an account with an online video distribution service like OneLoad.com (formerly TubeMogul), that will push your video message out to hundreds of popular video communities.

Many of these video sharing sites manually review and approve each video submission before it's posted, so it probably will take at least a few hours before all of your videos are up online.

Your computer may have come with a program for recording audio. If so, you can use that to record the audio for your video. Just play your slideshow presentation and use the audio recording program on your computer to put down your audio track following the script as you go.

Don't worry if it's not top-flight professional quality. Just speak slowly and clearly and enunciate your words. Avoid the urge to rush through the script. If for some reason your computer doesn't already have an audio recording tool, you can download a program such as Audacity. There are a lot of them available, most of them with free trials.

It's not unusual for people to dislike the way they sound on an audio recording because we aren't used to hearing our own voices the way other people hear them. Don't worry if you are unhappy with the way the audio for your video turned out.

If you truly hate it, you can always ask a friend to record the audio for you. Or you can hire a voiceover artist, but unless you are recording a commercial-grade video, this probably isn't worth the expense.

Try creating videos using both techniques. This will double your exposure and give you experience with different types of video production. Because video is quickly becoming the primary internet marketing platform, this experience will pay off.

You can post your videos on your web page, Facebook and even include a link to it on Twitter. Wherever you post it, however, don't forget to post a link to your site underneath your video. It's amazing that a lot of people forget this step!

Owning YouTube

YouTube is the biggest of the video sharing sites in North America, so if you don't post your videos on any other site, you should post it on YouTube. You can't literally own YouTube because it's already owned by Google (and they have more money than the Vatican), but there are some ways you can get a lot of viewers for your videos on YouTube.

Besides music videos, TV shows and movies, there are two kinds of videos that are immensely popular on YouTube: The how-to video and videos that are unusual.

If you post how-to videos, those that are part of a series tend to be more popular than those that stand alone. If you have a 10 minute video explaining how to make homemade ice cream, for example, you would get more visitors if you broke it into five 2-minute videos.

One quick way to get content up on YouTube is to record any seminars or webinars you give. Break your video into several separate files and create a video series that users of YouTube can subscribe to. This is a great way to build a following and increase your chances of having your video go viral.

How-to videos should provide valuable information that people can use to perform some task. You can feature your products and business if you want, but videos that are commercialized tend to be less popular than those that appear to be independent.

The second kind of video that is hugely popular on YouTube is those that are quirky and/or funny. Some of the most popular videos of all time on the site have featured people doing unusual yet interesting things.

Babies and young children doing and saying funny things are very popular on YouTube, as are people lip-syncing and animals. On YouTube, weird is revered. If it's appropriate for your product, try to come up with an idea that is wacky yet fascinating. If you hit the right tone, there are a huge number of viewers for these kinds of videos.

The Ratings Game: Yelp, Foursquare, Urban Spoon and Others

On the internet, everyone's a critic. Literally. Some of the more popular sites are those that allow members to post reviews and comments about businesses and the places they visit. Some of the most popular are:

Yelp

With more than 54 million unique visitors per month, this San Francisco-based user review and local search site is among the most popular. Users can post reviews about anything, from restaurants to dog parks to national parks. They also can search for certain kinds of businesses with defined geographic area. If you want to find a knife sharpening business in Sarasota, Florida, for example, Yelp can offer you options, along with customer reviews, maps, photos, hours of operation and other information.

Yelp does allow businesses to post advertisements and to be designated as "featured businesses". But because of the growing popularity of the site and others like it, most businesses spend more time playing defense than offense: Bad reviews on the site can be damaging.

Google Reviews

When searching Google for local business categories, a newer feature added to the search results are the Google reviews. Sometimes the reviews are taken from Google My Business reviews and other times from Zagat, which Google purchased back in 2011. Google controls about 80% of searches in the US and more like 95% of those from Europe. With that kind of exposure, Google reviews are a very powerful marketing tool when used correctly. You cannot post reviews about your own business but you can encourage your customers to post reviews about you.

Foursquare

Foursquare is a social networking site for mobile devices, such a smart phones. Members "check in" at various places they visit and are also linked to other users, and each can see the others check-ins. Each check-in awards the user points and sometimes "badges". The Foursquare user with the most check-ins at any particular place is named the "mayor" of that location. The app also allows users to leave comments, make recommendations and to send instant messages to other users.

Foursquare is a fun, youthful smart phone app that also has a competitive edge to it as members compete to collect the most badges and be named mayor of the most places.

Foursquare allows companies to provide discounts and freebies to members that check-in at their location. These can be effective marketing strategies for persuading new customers and regular customers to visit your business. Businesses also can create pages of tips and allow users to "follow" the company and receive exclusive tips and even special badges when they check-in at enough locations. Some restaurants and bars have even begun posting the Foursquare logo on their front window to encourage members to check-in there.

LinkedIn

LinkedIn is a social network that allows you to keep track and organize professional connections. Since 2003, LinkedIn has been helping business professionals keep track of current and former co-workers, find jobs, learn more about potential employers, arrange for professional references, and fill job vacancies.

For the internet marketer, LinkedIn is a great way to network with people and to make contact with other professionals. It's not as good a place to promote products as Twitter and Facebook, but it can be useful in developing long-term business relationships with others who can help promote your products and services.

Digg

Digg is one of the most popular of the "social news" sites that have developed in recent years. Users are able to post articles and links about things that of are interest to them. Other users can then like or dislike the articles. Those that are the most popular are pushed to the top of the Digg feed and those that are not fall to the bottom.

Digg is sort of like a combination of Google and Yelp, where users take over the role played by the search engine algorithm. It can be an effective way to promote your articles, blogs and websites and potentially increase traffic to your site by creating additional backlinks.

Flickr and Instgram

Flickr was the most popular of the photo sharing sites before Instagram came along. Users can upload photos or photo albums and even short videos to these sites, where they can be viewed by family and friends. Many businesses are using these sites to promote their products and services, however, and it can be an effective way to provide access to your company's catalogue or build your reputation online. They owe much of their success to their ease of use.

Wikipedia

Wikipedia is an online encyclopedia that is edited by its users. It has quickly become the go-to site for information for everyone on the web because it provides extensive basic information on every topic imaginable.

The downside is that because the content can be provided and edited by everybody, some of the veracity of its entries can come under scrutiny.

Still, there are business applications for Wikipedia that include creating an entry for your business that describes its products and services, its history and location, and its motivating mission statement.

Photos can also be uploaded onto Wikipedia pages. It could be a good way to help people find your business.

Skype

Skype provides video telephone and conferencing services for its 521 million users. It's free to download and Skype to Skype calls are also free. It is a great way to conduct business meetings and conferences without everybody having to travel to a single location, and its video ability makes it easy to give presentations. You can even load PowerPoint presentations onto it and include a voiceover.

Skype is quickly gaining in popularity as more and more businesses become aware of its benefits. It will certainly have a deep impact on business travel in the coming years, perhaps even on telecommuting.

As a traffic generating tool, it is important for your customers to know that you have Skype access because it will make many of them more willing to contact you directly. This can give you an opportunity to sell them additional products and improve your relationships without having to physically travel to their location.

Pinterest: It's Not Just for your Mother's Meatloaf Recipe

The internet is a fickle place and the fortunes of websites rise and fall. For example, MySpace just a few years ago was the most popular social networking site on the planet. Today it has few visitors and is co-owned by Justin Timberlake, who may rename it *MyEmptySpace* (just kidding, but Timberlake really does co-own it now).

However, when you're hot, you're hot. And one of the hottest websites right now is Pinterest. It's what is known as a social bookmarking site, or a place where users can create pages where they can post links to articles, web pages and other content that are of interest to them that they would like to share with others.

With Pinterest, users can "pin" links that interest them so that visitors can gain instant access to recommendations and referrals. Users can use preprogrammed page templates or design their own pages so that they can look any way they want.

Pinterest is an easy way to promote your web pages and products because it can be linked to your blog page, Twitter feed, Facebook page, LinkedIn page or just about any other site. Its popularity and influence continue to grow, making it a site that needs to be included in your internet marketing plan.

Seeking Sales on your Smartphone: Mobile SMS

People love text messaging because it's fast, easy and doesn't require actual contact with other people. Mobile

SMS (Short Message Service) is a marketing method that capitalizes on the popularity of texting by having businesses send texts promoting products or offering discounts to people's cell phones.

In some cases, the messages are sent to cell phone numbers the business purchased from a third party, sometimes the cell phone provider itself.

These types of spam messages can be a nuisance and are not generally appreciated by the recipient, so avoid this type of advertising.

A more effective Mobile SMS marketing campaign is to have customers opt-in to the service and voluntarily receive text messages from a business, usually in exchange for special offers or discounts. Given the popularity of texting and the fact that nearly everybody has a smart phone, this type of marketing is hugely popular.

SMS marketing programs are usually run off a short code, which are 5 or 6 digit numbers that have been assigned by all the mobile operators in a given country for the use of brand campaigns. Businesses can then use that short code as the text address for their marketing campaigns, such as "Text 'Event' to 54321 to receive updates and schedules for this week's Concert Events".

Leasing short codes generally costs between $500 and $1,000 per month, although some companies share short codes with other businesses to reduce costs. Another less expensive alternative is to simply run the service through the company's phone number.

Modern Modern Art: QR Codes

QR codes (Quick Response codes) are those black and white splotches that have begun showing up on advertisements and packaging. They are designed to be used with barcode type readers that can be downloaded onto any smart phone for free. When the user scans the QR code, in most cases they are immediately taken to the business's web page.

QR codes have the ability to contain more information than traditional bar codes and originally were used for inventory control in the Japanese automobile industry. But marketers soon realized that they can provide customers instant, effortless access to business's web pages. Consumers who scan QR codes usually are more likely to actually buy products than those using any other form of marketing path, such as sales pages or emails.

Besides marketing, businesses also have begun using QR codes for a lot of different applications, such as concert and sporting event ticketing, and offering coupons and discounts.

QR Codes can be created with a free app offered by Google and other websites. They can be embedded with a website URL, a text message, or links to anything or anywhere you want.

CHAPTER FIVE

How Does Your Garden Grow?

"The future of advertising is the Internet." – Bill Gates

Building any business is about building your list of customers. In the digital age, this usually means building your email subscription list. Once you have somebody's email address, you can send them special offers, discounts and other emails that promote your business. It's like a direct mail campaign but without the postage.

Just because you have somebody's email address, however, doesn't mean they are going to open your email.

Think about the number of emails you received just today. How many did you open? How many did you delete without reading them? Odds are there were more of the latter than the former.

Sending emails that nobody wants to read is a waste of time, both yours and theirs. The trick is to send emails that people can't wait to read and that they actually look forward to receiving. How is this possible? Two ways:

The first is by providing something people actually want, something that they consider high-value. What this is depends on the type of business you are promoting. It could be a monthly discount coupon, or perhaps a link to the latest installment of the instructional video series you created. It may be a chatty newsletter about what's been happening in your business.

The second way is to make your emails highly personal. Talk about your family and the good people who work for you. Include lots of pictures and links to videos.

Give your customers access into your life and the life of your business. In most cases, their curiosity will be enough to get them to open it.

A good strategy is to put yourself in your customer's shoes. If you were your customer, what kind of email would you want to receive from your business?

A coupon for a free ice cream cone on your birthday?

An entry into a sweepstakes to win a new car?

A report on how your kids' hockey team did in the sectionals?

A video of you singing a karaoke version of the Allman Brothers' "Tied to the Whipping Post"?

If you want your customers to open your emails, you have to make sure they are fun, contain high-value content, and reach people on a personal level.

Accomplish these goals and you can dramatically decrease the number of times people delete your emails without reading them.

Mine's Bigger: Cultivating Your Existing Customer Base

Before you can send your fun, cool emails to your customers, you need to capture their email addresses.

There are a number of effective ways to do this.

You Can Ask Them

Train your sales staff to ask your customers for their email address when they talk to your customers on the phone. This is especially effective for businesses that routinely ask for a call-back number, such as restaurants, theaters, service companies, and consultants. You can also tell existing customers that you are updating your customer list to include emails. *You are, right?*

You Can Incentivize Them

You can print your email address at the bottom of your sales receipt and during checkout invite your customers to participate in an online survey about the quality of their service experience. Participants are automatically enrolled in a monthly drawing for a cash prize. When they log in to the survey page, ask for their email address.

You Can Ask For Their Help

Send out an email encouraging your existing subscribers to forward your email to a friend. If your content is strong enough and your customers have bought in to the community you have created, many will.

You Can Offer a Discount

Start a free customer loyalty club in which customers who join can receive special offers and exclusive discounts. On the application form, include a space for them to give you their email address. With the proper financial incentive and with no cost or risk, most customers will happily join.

You can then issue your customers a card embedded with a QR code on it to identify them as members, as well as a smaller version they can put on their keychain. This card is then read with the QR reader at checkout. It's a good way to track customers' purchases and preferences so you can market specific products and services via future emails.

You Can Capture It From Incoming Emails

When people send you emails, add their email address to your subscription list. It doesn't get any easier than that.

Has Anyone Seen My Autoresponder?

The most important tool you will need to complete this conversion is an autoresponder, which are programs that automatically handle much of the administrative duties of maintaining your email marketing campaign. Autoresponders will automatically send out your emails to the people on your list, capture email addresses from prospects responding to your squeeze pages, distribute your free giveaways, and collect analytics so that you can measure the success of your operation.

Autoresponders can be programmed to send out a series of emails to the people on your list – or to select subsets of people – based on a frequency and schedule that you determine.

This is important because marketing research has shown that most people don't buy products promoted by email marketing until they have received multiple emails about the product:

What Market Research Tells Us

- 16 Percent will buy products after only one or two emails.

- 34 Percent after three or four emails.

- 34 Percent after five or six.

- 16 Percent after seven or more emails (as well as the passage of considerable time between the first and last).

As a result, you will need eight to ten emails to pre-load into your autoresponder program if you want to maximize the sales potential for your products. Each email should gradually build on the information presented in the preceding one to make your product more irresistible to your customers.

Try not to be repetitive. If you don't have anything new to say, don't send an email just for the sake of repetition.

If you are having a hard time coming up with new ideas, try running a Google search on your niche or other hot topics that you think your customers might like. Write up an article on the topic and include the original link, as well as a link to your web page, of course.

This can be an effective method to keep your customers engaged without repeatedly sending them the same message.

You also will need to determine the frequency for your emails.

If you send eight in one day, for example, your customers are unlikely to buy and more likely to opt out of your list. Unless your content is killer, anything more than twice per week is likely to turn people off. In most cases, one or two emails per week are ideal.

You also can set up your autoresponder so that it flags addresses after a certain number of failed delivery attempts. This is helpful in cleaning up your list and keeping it up to date.

Another great idea is to program your autoresponder so that it sends your email out in both plaint text and HTML.

This will make it easier to accommodate different loading speeds depending on what types of programs your customers are using. Always have the autoresponder send every email to an address you own first – in both HTML and text – so you can see exactly what your customers will see before it officially gets sent off.

Most autoresponders include the option to automatically insert your customer's name in the body of the email. This makes it seem like you are personally sending the email to your individual subscribers.

Depending on the sophistication of your autoresponder, you can mine a lot of data about your email marketing campaign.

Every program will tell you how many emails were successfully sent, but more sophisticated autoresponders also can give you analytics on:

How many of your customers actually opened your email.

How many clicked through to your landing page (CTA).

How many deleted your email without reading it.

How many were sent to dead addresses.

How long it took between the time the email arrived and the time it was opened or deleted.

All of this information is helpful to you in fine-tuning your email marketing campaign. Patterns will quickly emerge that tell you what types of emails your customers liked, and which ones turn them off.

You can test out different email marketing strategies by splitting your list into two or more subsets, then sending out slightly different versions of the same email message. The differences don't have to be dramatic. For example, you can try using different subject headings, fonts and colors. Keep track of which ones get the best response, then design your future emails based on your customers' preferences.

Mama's Got a Squeeze Page, Daddy Never Sleeps at Night

A squeeze page is a web page separate from your main web page that is designed to capture visitors' email addresses. Usually, it offers something of value – a free report, an informational video, an eBook – in exchange for their email address.

Whatever you give away should offer something of value related to your product niche. For example, if you own a driving range, you can offer visitors the free report, "Top 10 Tips to Improving Your Short Game." All visitors need to do is to give you their email address so that you know where to send the report. Passionate consumers such as avid golfers are always looking for ways to improve their game, and will happily receive your article, especially if it's free.

Once they enter their email address into the box, your autoresponder automatically sends a copy of your report to their email address, and you instantaneously have the email address of a potential customer who is an enthusiastic fan of the types of products you sell.

Questionnaires, Polls and Contests

Building your list can be fun for both you and your customers when you use questionnaires, polls and contests. The response rate usually is quite high because people love to give their opinions about things. Offer your customers the opportunities and in most cases they will comply.

Questionnaires are used for more serious product research and tend to be more in-depth. If you want a detailed analysis about the effectiveness of a particular advertising campaign or about what your customers feel about the layout of your store, for example, you can either hire a consultant to conduct a poll for you or try to do it yourself, although this is not recommended due to the time requirement.

When commissioning your questionnaire, make sure your consultant understands that the primary purpose is to capture email addresses, although the marketing data also will be useful.

Polls are a simple, fun way to engage your customers. Post a single question on your web page or even inside your business about some fun topic, such as favorite products. This can be done once per week, or even every day. Anything related to your local sports team is sure to get a lot of responses.

If you are using website programs such as WordPress to design and maintain your web pages, they have free plug-ins you can use to insert polls onto your pages. Make sure to include an opt-in box to capture email addresses because building your subscriber list is the primary objective.

Contests are a fun way to get your customers excited about your business. Prizes don't necessarily have to be anything of high value, such as a car or vacation trips. They can be something silly that costs little or nothing, such as a personalized parking space right next to your businesses for one lucky winner, a 30-second shopping spree in your store, or being designated as the business's "favorite customer" and having their picture posted on the wall for a month. Entry forms include a spot where participants give you their email address.

The point is to build your email list while creating a culture that's fun and exciting for your customers. The more your customers enjoy doing business with you, the more loyal they will remain.

Asking Your Customers to Help You

One way to get more loyal customers to your business is by allowing them to influence the way it is run. Obviously, you aren't going to leave any major decisions in the hands of your customers, but you can certainly ask them to help you with such non-critical issues as which color to paint the walls or which new logo they prefer.

Asking people for help is one of the best ways to create trust bonds with them. And in most cases, people will respond, especially if they have genuinely bought in to the community that you have created around your business

Organize a charitable project and ask your customers to pitch in. It can be cleaning up a vacant lot, planting trees in a local park or even a toy drive. This has the dual benefit of helping the community and building your business's reputation as being a caring partner with it. Asking your customers to be included in this kind of project will strengthen your bonds with them and advance your objective of making them raving fans.

We're Going to Need a Bigger Fishbowl!

Collecting business cards is a fast, effective way of building your community among the businesses in your area. The simplest way is to buy an inexpensive fishbowl and invite your customers to drop their business cards into it for a chance to win some modest prize, such as a gift certificate or store credit.

Once per month, empty out the fishbowl and choose one winner. If you include a message on the fishbowl that says you will also be collecting any email addresses printed on the business cards, you can add them to your subscribers list. Just be sure to get permission first.

There's a lot you can do with business cards. Many people are oddly proud of them and appreciate the opportunity to use them for something. Some bars and restaurants invite patrons to staple their business cards to the ceiling or to a designated wall. This allows the business card owners to point out their business cards to their friends and co-workers, hopefully bringing more people back to your business.

Referral Incentives

You can ask your customers to drive new business for you by offering a referral incentive. This usually takes the form of a discount or premium in exchange for referring a friend, relative or someone else.

Referral incentives help build the community of your business because they require your customers to essentially vouch for your business. When they recommend your business to somebody else, they are putting themselves on the line in a way, so they have something at stake in your success.

Plus, people who are referred by a friend to your business already have a positive expectation about your business when they walk in the door or visit your website. A referral program allows you to nurture new customers while at the same time solidifying your bonds with your existing customers.

CHAPTER SIX

Life Lessons Learned from Jimmy Kimmel

"We are all now connected by the Internet, like neurons in a giant brain." - Stephen Hawking

Jimmy Kimmel is a late night talk show host whose program "Jimmy Kimmel Live" is broadcast long after prime time is over. He safely avoided the late night wars that pitted bigger names such as retired hosts David Letterman and Jay Leno against each other. His show has neither the highest nor the lowest ratings. But it is almost certain that Jimmy Kimmel will be able to continue to produce his show for as long as he wants without ever fearing cancellation.

That's because Jimmy Kimmel's program is a marvelous example of cross-promotion. Its ties to its sponsors are much more obvious than the other late night talk shows. And the program is owned by The Walt Disney Company, which also owns the network it is broadcast on, ABC, as well as ESPN, so the program is constantly promoting Disney products such as movies, TV shows, and sporting events.

The program has tie-ins to many of ABC's most popular programs. For example, during the "Dancing with the Stars" seasons, the teams voted off each week are rushed to Kimmel's studio in the Egyptian Theater on Hollywood Boulevard to discuss their experience with Jimmy, and watch as their dancing shoes were ceremoniously burned in a trash barrel outside.

And the first segment of every show just before the opening credits is devoted every night to a comedy skit that is focused on a particular sponsor's product. While critics may claim this is blending the line between art and commerce; for the viewers it's entertaining, and for the program it's additional revenue.

Finally, Kimmel himself occasionally appeared on other talk shows, such as Late Night with David Letterman and Howard Stern's show. These are not my competition, he seems to be saying, and there's plenty of room for all of us.

The point is that Jimmy Kimmel has created an effective way to use his business to seamlessly cross-promote other businesses. Most viewers to the program aren't aware or don't care that the purpose of these is to promote products – whether they are Disney movies, music, or orange juice – they just enjoy the show's entertainment value.

Your business can learn from the example of Jimmy Kimmel's cross-marketing. When you broaden your circle to include other businesses as well as customers, you increase the opportunity to gain exposure for your business as well. And, like Jimmy Kimmel, you essentially guarantee that you will never be cancelled.

Building Buzz: Cross Marketing Business Partner Relationship Building

Frequently, business owners develop a kind of siege mentality: They want to protect their business and retain their customers so they view other businesses as enemies. This can lead to a lot of bad things, such as speaking critically of other businesses, being secretive about your operations and revenues, and generally poisoning the business community.

What a waste of time.

Like late night talk shows, there's usually plenty of room for everybody in the marketplace. And by working with other businesses, rather than against them, you can share your knowledge and experience and improve operations for both businesses.

The first place to start is simply getting to know your neighbors. Are you in an area where there are a lot of other small businesses, such as a shopping mall, a strip mall or a central shopping district?

Take an afternoon and walk around introducing yourself to the other business owners. Be friendly and outgoing.

Ask for advice about a particular issue you may be having or find some area of commonality, such as parking issues.

Let other business owners into the community you have created around your business. There may be opportunities to cross promote your businesses.

For example, if you own a shoe store, you definitely want to get to know the podiatrists in your area. Not only can they recommend your business to their patients, they may also be willing to give a talk at your store for your customers, increasing their exposure as well.

Join your local chamber of commerce or merchants association and get to know the other business owners in your community. If your area doesn't have a business association, start one.

The information that business owners can share with each other can make everybody's business work more efficiently, not to mention the influence you can enjoy in matters of public policy.

Attend every networking event you can, even if it is not directly related to your industry. As a business owner, the more people you know in your area, the better off you will be because you never know when a particular contact is going to pay off.

If your business is in an area where there aren't any marketing events, host one at your business one night per month.

Think about ways you can get other businesses involved in your business.

Can you bring in other business owners as guest speakers?

Can you feature their products in your store?

Do your products or services complement each other?

Can you sponsor a joint community event, such as 5K run or a neighborhood block party?

Anything you can do in partnership with other business owners in your community will help you build your own reputation, and also create relationships which can help you later.

It's even worthwhile to build business-to-business relationships with your direct competitors. After all, it's business, not warfare. You may be competing for the same customer base, but you both deal with the exact same issues every day so there's an opportunity to help each other out.

Make your tent as big as possible and invite as many people under it as you can and you can share in each other's success.

How to Make Friends and Influence Your Joint Ventures

It's nice to be important, but it's important to be nice. The relationships you make with other business people in your community can not only help you build a support group to fall back on when you need advice and guidance, but they can even help your business succeed by joining you in a joint venture.

One benefit of building good relationships with other business owners in your area is that they may be able to provide capital for projects you want to try but may not be able to afford on your own. Joint ventures are a great way to create new businesses without assuming all the risk on your own.

If you have gotten to know other business owners and they are familiar with your sound business practices, they may be willing to go into business with you on a new project, or even invest in your existing business if that's what you want. Because you are both already doing business in the same community, you already both have something at stake in its success.

Conversely, if you have excess capital and another business owner you trust approaches you with a joint venture idea, you should consider buying into it. At the very least, there's the opportunity to gain access to their customer base. At the best, the new business can be very successful.

Joint ventures allow two or more companies to team up to form a new business or accomplish a specific task. They allow business owners to take advantage of each other's strengths. For example, one business owner may have a lot of experience in building online businesses and the other company may have a great idea for a new web-based company but lacks the start-up capital.

Joint ventures can be faster to get up and running than single-owner businesses because responsibilities can be shared and you can fall back on the resources of both companies – such as a payroll department or technology – rather than trying to build everything yourself from scratch.

Entering into a joint venture with another business owner also can give you access to new markets and even new customers. Many joint ventures take the form of a wholesaler or retailer distributing a manufacturing company's products. Or the two investor businesses can combine their email subscription lists.

Sometimes joint ventures are formed because one company has something the other company needs, such as a new technology or access to overseas markets. Joint ventures also allow you to leverage the relationships and goodwill already established by both partners to the benefit of all.

For your business, a joint venture with somebody else also is a great way to acquire new leads and have access to your partner's customer base with no effort or cost. It also can give you a way to increase the capacity of your business without substantial additional capital investment.

You also may be able to offer your customers additional products and services as a result of your joint venture relationship. Remember: The more you can offer your customers, the more valuable you are to them.

Like any business decision, it's important to look before you leap into a joint venture partnership. You want to make sure you find a partner you can work with and start with a clear understanding of what the objectives and responsibilities of each party will be.

Both sides also should bring approximately the same amount of expertise, investment or assets to the venture; otherwise it can lead to problems later.

Don't Follow Leaders, Watch the Parking Meters: The New Business Paradigm

The way business is conducted globally has undergone a remarkable change in a very short period of time. Old business models are failing and although success is never guaranteed; it does tend to favor those businesses that are bold and innovative.

Creating products that customers can't live without is one easy pathway to success, but not every business is lucky enough to be able to do that. Sometimes you're just selling shoes.

In today's business environment, being conservative isn't an option. Unless you have very deep pockets, waiting around for business conditions without developing any new innovation is a good way to go broke. Now more than ever, risk is rewarded and those companies bold enough to take the biggest chances often reap the biggest rewards.

Fear of failure usually is the biggest obstacle to making bold decisions for your company, but being afraid is rarely the right answer.

No one wants to go broke, but if you want your company to succeed, you have to make the brave decisions and you can't be afraid to fail.

How can you find the breakthrough ideas that can put your business over the top?

There's an old saying from the Book of Ecclesiastes: "Nihil Novi Sub Sole" which means "There's nothing new under the sun." Everything that can be done has been done at some time and in some fashion. When you want to learn how to drive a car, do you have to chisel a wheel out of rock or go work the assembly line at Ford's Rouge River plant? No, you just get in the car and go!

It's the same in business. If you want new ideas for your business, you don't have to start from the beginning. Instead, build on the foundations that businesses before you have created. Thanks to the World Wide Web, you have unlimited global access to companies just like yours on every continent. Spend some research time seeing what other businesses are doing and then borrow all of their best ideas for your own.

Another fantastic resource is right under your nose. Your employees know better than anybody what is done well at your business and what can be improved. But if they are afraid to say anything for fear of reprimand, they aren't going to stick their neck out to help you. When you create the community that is your business, make sure it includes a culture in which innovation is encouraged and even rewarded.

Solicit ideas from your employees. Ask them their opinion and assure them that they won't be penalized for being honest. It may take some time for them to trust you, but be persistent and you will be rewarded with keen insights from the people who are in the best position to have them. As an additional incentive, you could even offer to share with them additional revenues their big idea brings in, with some sort of cap, of course.

Your customers bring a different perspective of your business than you have, so you always want to keep lines of communication with them open.

If you are the owner, make sure you take the time to get on the front lines of your business and speak directly to your customers daily. Don't depend solely on what your managers or supervisors are telling you because they have a vested interest in keeping bad news away from you. You will find out more by spending one hour on the sales floor of your business than you will in a month of staff meetings.

If you want to expand your business you may need to expand your product line. Can you offer your existing products in different color and styles?

What sorts of products complement your existing product line?

What about launching an entirely new line altogether?

When you diversify your offering to your customers, you give them the opportunity to spend more money with your business.

Another way to make more money is to find ways to increase sales to your existing customers. Even if you can't expand your product line, you can still boost your sales by selling more of your existing product or service to the customers you already have, such as through volume discounts.

If you offer one widget for $10, for example, why not bundle 5 for $45? As long as your costs are covered, it can only result in increased sales revenues.

If your creativity has hit a wall and you find yourself running out of fresh ideas, bring in an outsider who can take a fresh look at your business.

This can be a trusted friend, business associate or family member.

If you want to make your business appeal more to younger people, ask your intern for advice or bring in some teenagers or college students and ask for their advice. They are sure to have a lot of ideas and can give insight into a market you probably wouldn't have been able to penetrate otherwise.

If your budget allows it, you could even hire a consultant or an outside firm to analyze your company and offer suggestions for improvement.

Usually, the money these types of consultants can generate more than compensates for the expense of hiring them.

Target markets outside of your primary market.

If your business is wholesale, consider starting a retail operation.

If you are retail, there may be an opportunity to sell wholesale.

If you sell clothes for children, consider adding a maternity line.

If you own a sporting goods store, perhaps you could launch a new hunting or fishing guide business, or enter into a joint venture with area guides to promote their services in exchange for a sales commission.

Increase your personal profile in your community. Customers always prefer putting a face with a business. If you spend your days working in a back office, nobody is going to know who you are. But if you schedule public speaking engagements at your local library or before your local service clubs, you can begin to build your reputation and open new avenues to promote your business. Volunteer to write a column for your local newspaper or call your local radio station's talk show and ask if they would be willing to have you on as a guest.

Consider opening one or more new locations, or even selling franchises of your business. If your business is successful in its current scale, in all likelihood it can be successful on a bigger scale. By franchising your business, you don't have to worry about building capital, hiring and training staff, buying equipment, leasing space or any of the other endless start-up concerns. You can collect the franchise fee and make sure your buyer is maintaining your business's high standards.

Do you own trademarks that you can license?

Do you own a recognizable brand?

Try having some t-shirts, coffee mugs, jackets or other accessories made up with your logo and sell them in your stores and on your website. Start with a small order at first then bump up your order and get a volume discount once sales begin to build.

If you are a new business, be prepared to reinvest your revenues back into your business until operations really get off the ground. Depending on what type of business you are in, you should be prepared to break even or even lose money for at least the first year or two. You'll need to devote whatever income you have to promoting your business through marketing, investing in infrastructure, and compensating your best employees so that they stick with you through the tough early days.

The new business environment requires a new business paradigm. Conservative, slow-to-change businesses that are afraid to take chances aren't going to survive. But companies that are quick to try new approaches, embrace fresh ideas, and actively seek out the most innovative ideas, product lines and sales platforms, stand to reap enormous rewards.

The Traveling Party

Being successful in the 21st century business environment requires more than simply great products or even an effective marketing program.

To convert customers into raving fans requires creating a community around your business. It necessitates building a culture that your customers want to be a part of.

Think about your business as creating a village, one that includes people from all walks of life, each of whom has something unique and valuable to contribute.

What kind of community would you like to live in? Would you rather live in a community that was cold and uninviting, or one in which everyone was made to feel valued and where every day events were celebrated? In your community, the milestones of your employees' lives – birthdays, weddings, engagements, and babies – are important to everybody, including your customers. Your community is a place filled with joy and love, and where people care about each other and watch out for each other's well-being.

This type of culture does not happen organically, however. It's up to you to create it. As the business owner, all of your employees are looking to you for clues as to how to behave and interact with other employees and with customers.

If you are introverted and shy, they will be as well. If you have a short temper, expect to see explosions on your sales floor. But if you are caring, loving and show a genuine interest in other people and nurture their success, this type of attitude will set the tone for your community and your employees will do the same.

Then, when you create something that people want to become a part of, two things will happen:

Customers will want to be a part of your community and will actually look forward to your emails, sales calls and promotions.

Your employee turnover will decrease to next to zero because no one will want to leave.

Your business doesn't end at your property line. Its scope includes your entire community and it goes wherever you go. As the living face of your business, it's important for you to be an active part of the community you live and work in. Be a joiner: If you are a spiritual person, consider becoming more active in your church. Join civic organizations and participate in their meetings and events. Try to become an officer in those groups and let others know you would be willing to serve on committees and boards.

Increase your public profile by attending grand openings and ribbon cuttings. Socialize with other business leaders and office holders. The more often you can get your picture in the paper, the better off your business community will be.

When you meet new people, listen to what they have to say. Don't be the one talking all the time. Be open to all ideas, no matter how off the wall. Most importantly, be aggressively friendly - go out of your way to make people feel welcome and at ease - and encourage your employees to be the same. If you set a consistent example, they will follow it.

CHAPTER SEVEN

I DO Give a Damn about My Bad Reputation

"Computers and the Internet have made it really easy to rant. It's made everyone overly opinionated." - Scott Weiland

Like many young people, when you were a kid you may have not cared what other people thought about you. This type of rebelliousness is a natural part of growing up. But somewhere along the way, whether we like it or not, all that changes.

What people think about you is very important, especially if you are a business owner. What you do and say reflects not just on you, but on your business and on everybody who works there and even on your customers.

That's why it's important to be not only friendly and outgoing, but politically correct as well.

Is it worth losing a large chunk of your business and alienating half of your customer base by being vocal about your opinions on such things as politics, religion and other hair-trigger topics?

In most cases, a better plan is to save your thoughts on controversial issues for your closest friends and family and be as neutral as possible in your public life.

Even if you are as meek as a lamb and never comment on anything more controversial than the weather report, your reputation and that of your business can still be damaged by other people, especially in the digital age when everybody has access to hundreds of Facebook friends, Twitter followers, and LinkedIn associates. And then there are sites such as Yelp and Foursquare, where users can share their opinion about your business with thousands of strangers whose sole exposure to your business may be that particular review.

The best defense is a good offense, so by maintaining the highest quality standards and requiring your employees to do the same, you can ensure that you are providing the best customer service experience possible, giving your customers little to complain about. Still, it's impossible to personally monitor every interaction.

Each of your employees is your representative when they interact with a customer, so it's up to you to make sure they have a clear understanding of what your expectations are. Codify it as much as possible: Script what you want your employees to say and specify how you want them to behave. Incentivize them to do a good job with recognition programs such as employee of the month awards and cash prizes for superior work.

There's an old saying in management: If you expect, inspect. Once you create your quality standards, make sure there's a mechanism in place that measures them. Require your supervisors and managers to monitor employee/customer interactions and to submit regular evaluations both to you and to the employees. This kind of diligence is the best way to improve your chances of having high-quality customer experiences.

Wait, What? Reputation Monitoring

Even if you drill your employees night and day on the details of the customer interaction you want, in the end people are only human and eventually somebody will goof up and a customer will leave your business unhappy.

Given the high number of web-based outlets for unhappy customers to vent their frustrations, it's more likely than not that your business will get a bad review somewhere.

It's no longer like the old days when a customer would write a letter to the company president. Today, the minute they walk out your door, before they can even get to their car, they are typing up a nasty review on their smart phone and posting it out for the world to read.

It's vital that you know what people are saying about your business. It's a good idea to run a search for your business on Google, Bing and Yahoo frequently, preferably every day. If you don't have time, assign the task to one of your managers.

In most cases, if there is a new comment, the search engines will rank it near the top of the results page for your company name. You also should search sites that frequently include reviews of businesses like yours. For example, if you own a restaurant or hotel, you want to look at Yelp and Urban Spoon regularly to see what people are saying.

Best Practices for a Raw Deal

When you find a bad review, the first most important thing to do is to find out what caused it. Did the reviewer have a legitimately bad experience and if so, why? When you identify the breakdown you can repair it for next time. Maybe an employee was having a bad day and said something they shouldn't have said. If so, have your managers counsel the employee on what they did wrong so that he or she understands how to do better next time. If it has happened more than once or twice, it may be necessary to use steps of progressive discipline so that you can coach the employee to success or manage them out.

The problem may have been caused by equipment failure or a defective product, both of which can be addressed and fixed. Whatever the cause of the breakdown, it's important to identify it and correct it as soon as possible so that one bad review doesn't turn into five, ten or twenty. If that happens, you have a real problem on your hands.

Correcting the problem is only half the response. The other half is winning back the customer. If the comment was posted on a social media site or a social comment site, send the person who posted a direct message. Keep it brief: Identify yourself as the business owner and ask if they would be willing to contact you to discuss their experience. You don't know who else is going to see your message or what the person who posted is going to do with it, so you want to keep it as brief and neutral as possible.

Remember: Anytime something is sent over the internet, it is there forever. If you make the mistake of sending a sarcastic remark or a snide comment, you can pretty much expect it to go viral.

Instead, use the "60 Minutes" rule: Never do, say or write anything that you wouldn't be willing to have broadcast on CBS "60 Minutes". In most cases, it will come back to haunt you.

If that customer calls you back, you'll have the opportunity make things right. If they don't respond to your first message, try again so they know you are sincere.

If they contact you, try to get the complete story about exactly what went wrong. Many times their description will be completely different than the story you got from your own employees. Simply listen to what they have to say. Don't make any judgements or comments, just get the facts.

You want to make sure you apologize for their bad experience. You didn't have this type of thing in mind when you put in all the hard work creating the culture of your business.

If appropriate, offer the customer something to compensate them for their experience:

If you own a restaurant, ask if you can send them a gift certificate for a free dinner for two.

If you own another kind of business, do whatever you can to make it right.

This part is very important: If they accept your apology, nicely ask if they would be willing to remove their review from whatever website they posted it on. Explain that their experience is not typical of the way your customers are treated and assure them that you have taken steps to make sure it doesn't happen again. Let them know that their bad review might be the only thing some people ever read about your business and you don't want them to get a mistaken impression.

In most cases, this will be enough and the customer will agree to pull their review down and the problem is solved. Avoid coupling whatever you offer with a request they remove their review as it might come off as a quid pro quo situation, which will either make them even angrier or inspire them to ask for more from you in return for pulling it. It would also be unethical.

If they refuse to remove the review, thank them for accepting your apology and end the conversation on a friendly note. If it's only one review, odds are it won't adversely affect your business very much. And if your business has lots of bad reviews, you've got bigger problems to deal with anyway.

Defense and Protection Management

On social comment and social media websites, the vast majority of posts are from actual customers who are expressing their opinions about their experience at your business. But there is still a small percentage that perhaps has an axe to grind with you or more likely one of your employees, or perhaps a misguided competitor who is trying to use the internet to damage your business.

If you feel your business has been unfairly targeted by a review, a Tweet or any other kind of online comment, you do have some options.

If your request to the poster to remove the comment is rejected, most operators of social media sites will take it down if you explain the situation. They won't help you if you have multiple complaints from many different customers, but if one person obviously has a grudge against your business and has posted a particularly virulent review or a series of nasty posts; in most cases they will remove them from their website. After all, they have nothing to gain from damaging your business.

If they refuse, however, you may want to have your legal department give them a call, but definitely don't start from that aggressive of a position. It's always better to give people the opportunity to do the right thing on their own.

He Said/She Said: Social Mentions and Reviews Management

As social comment websites become more popular, learning how to manage your business's online reputation takes on increasing importance. There are even companies today whose entire business model is built upon protecting their clients' online reputations.

There are other businesses that actually hire people to write positive reviews about their businesses, which many rightfully consider an unethical practice. As a business owner, you need to decide what's right for your business. But this probably wouldn't pass the "60 Minutes" test.

A better, more ethical idea is to encourage your customers to rate their experience on your business at one of the social comment websites. If you select just one, it becomes easier to manage.

If you've done a good job of creating a culture that your customers willingly buy into, you can expect to receive many glowing reviews and recommendations.

At the same time, you can further encourage your customers to "Like" you on Facebook and follow you on Twitter, thus covering all of your social media in one fell swoop.

Once you receive a number of positive reviews, you can use these as part of your marketing plan. Always retweet positive comments on Twitter. You can pull quotes off of Yelp or other sites and use them in your advertising and marketing materials and also post them on your Facebook and Twitter pages.

In fact, many companies today have created positions whose sole responsibility is managing their social media, publicizing positive comments and addressing negative ones.

Social media is going to be with us for a long time, and as more people gain access to these sites, their usage is only going to increase. Learning to manage your company's reputation online is going to take on increasing importance in the coming years, especially as people abandon traditional research tools and use the faster, easier and more efficient tools of the internet to find products and services.

The Complaint Department

The first and best way to avoid customer complaints from going public is to make sure that your customers have nothing to complain about. When you focus your energies on creating and maintaining world-class customer service, it becomes much easier to manage your online reputation. Still, occasionally things will go wrong.

The second best way to avoid customer complaints from going public is to address and correct them before your customer leaves your business. Once they are out your door, it becomes much more difficult to conduct damage control. The key to catching customer problems before they leave and become worse is having effective managers. You pay your managers to ensure that your business is running smoothly in your absence. That means your employees are doing what they are supposed to be doing, that your people have the tools they need to do their jobs, and that your facility looks perfect all the time.

It is also the manager's job to observe the way your employees are interacting with your customers and to make sure that the quality standards you created are being followed. If yours is a brick and mortar business, good managers can tell when something is wrong simply by looking at the customer's face. When a customer's head appears to be on a pivot, as they are looking around for someone or something, it usually indicates a problem. If your manager can intercede and correct the problem immediately, there's usually no need for your customer to leave angry or upset enough to post a negative review on the internet.

Your manager is your complaint department. One of the key reasons you hired them is to handle problems, or anticipate problems before they can occur. In most cases, what unhappy customers want most is an empathetic person to whom they can express their frustration about their experience at your business. Your manager can soothe their hurt feelings and all will be well again.

If, however, despite all your efforts to nurture a positive and inspiring culture for your business it keeps getting bad reviews, the problem probably doesn't lie with your employees. After all, they are just doing what they are told or allowed to do. In most cases, the problem is inadequate supervision. Its human nature: If people aren't held accountable, they will fail to meet your expectations.

As the business owner, ultimately your managers report to you. In the same way that you expect your employees to adhere to your customer service standards, you need your managers to adhere to your supervisory standards. Make sure they understand what your expectations are. In the same way that they observe and evaluate your employees, it's up to you to observe and evaluate your managers.

No one likes to work in an environment where steps of progressive discipline are the primary motivating factor, although this is a common practice in a union environment. You are diligent about creating a community for your business that appreciates both your employees and your customers, a business that is also a community that values and encourages people's contribution to your success.

This type of oppressive system runs counter to that concept. Still, you've got to do whatever you need to in order to protect your business. The best option is to give people every opportunity to succeed and make every effort to coach them to success. Still, occasionally things just aren't going to work out and you will need to make some hard choices.

The Customer is Always Right, Right?

In dealing with customer service issues, overkill is better. Usually, customers won't complain unless they have a legitimate reason: Something in the customer service experience broke down. In other cases, customers complain because of something they perceived or misinterpreted: An overheard comment, a look or glance. It doesn't always make sense.

Regardless, if they are customers in your business and they have a problem, then you have a problem. It is much easier to fix it before they leave than to try to chase them down afterwards, especially if they publish something unkind about your business online.

The customer, being the paying party, gets the benefit of the doubt. Just as all ties go to the runner in baseball, all disputes should go to the customer. In a very few cases, a customer may simply be trying to get something for nothing or is causing a fuss for a reason unrelated to their actual experience in your business. Even in these cases, it's easier and better for your business to give the customer whatever they need to appease them than to dig in your heels and get into a confrontation with them, especially if your interaction is in view of other customers.

It's not always easy to back down when you believe you are right, but for the sake of your business, it's often the best option.

Obviously, if someone is trying to steal from you or do something illegal, then you should call the police and let them handle it. But in most cases, as long as you don't give away the store, you are better off appeasing your customer. In many cases, if you do an effective job making things right, those very same customers can become your biggest fans.

Finally, if you want to get your employees to buy into the community you are trying to make your business into, one of the fastest ways to accomplish this is to empower them.

One way to do so is to give them the authority to make things right for your customers without first requiring approval from their manager or supervisor, although they should notify their direct report supervisor after the fact. You also want to make your employees clearly understand the limits to what they can comp.

This has the dual effect of making your employees feel like they have a stake in the success of your business, and impressing your customers by the fact that you trust your employees enough to make those kinds of decisions.

Polishing Your Reputation

As the owner of your business, you have a lot of responsibilities. You have a lot of big decisions to make every day and there are many people who are depending on your making the right decisions for their livelihood.

People are looking to you for leadership. This means that you have to live your life in a bubble. Everything you say and do will be scrutinized by your employees and even your customers. It may not be fair, but as the leader of your business, the more authority you have, the greater the responsibility.

People may not always like to be told what to do, but they still want you to lead them. And they will love you if you can inspire them, both with your words and with your actions. It's a lot of responsibility and one that should be taken seriously, but the rewards go far beyond financial.

Your business is an extension of who you are. If you are a genuinely caring and nurturing person, then the community you are creating out of your business will thrive. By treating everybody fairly and with respect, you can inspire your employees to do the same and to give their best to your customers every day.

As the business owner, you don't stop being the boss once you leave your building. For your employees, that's who you are. They have no idea what you were like in high school or what fraternity you joined in college. The only person they know is "You the Boss." So you need to pay as much attention to your reputation outside of work as you do on the job. Be as thoughtful of what you do and say outside of work as you are when at the office.

Being the owner requires you to be the grownup all the time.

Although you probably won't have a lot of time, you can help build your reputation by becoming involved with a charitable organization. By volunteering your time to help out on projects or serve on a board or steering community, you can give back to your community and at the same time enhance your reputation.

Getting your company involved with a charity is a great way to motivate your employees as well. They will feel proud to work for a business that is caring and giving to people in need. Plus it can help your company's reputation in your customers' eyes.

Finally, you might consider running for public office. You can use the same leadership qualities you use to run your business to help your community. If you have no political experience, you can start small by running for a school council seat or a minor elected position. You probably will want to avoid a position that requires a huge time commitment, such as mayor or congressman, unless that is your ambition.

CHAPTER EIGHT

Sustaining the Village: Love Letters to the Future

"The story of the Internet is this incredibly strong, exciting change." - James Daly

The future of business is being determined today, right now. The growing migration from brick and mortar businesses to e-commerce has caused many changes to how businesses are run and will continue to sculpt the business landscape in new and interesting ways.

The old business models are dead. Cautious, conservative decision making is no longer rewarded with slow and steady growth; it's answered with obsolescence and shrinking profits.

In the 21st century, changes come much more quickly than ever before and those businesses that are best able to make adaptations quickly are the ones that will stay viable longer.

This isn't necessarily a bad thing. These changes enable you to create a new model for your business. While this model is just as committed to the objectives of generating ever-increasing revenues and expansion of market share, it also assumes that those objectives can only be achieved now if everyone is allowed to participate in the conversation.

Leadership structures are more horizontal now, rather than the vertical chains of command of the old business model. Yet the 21st century business owners have more tools at their disposal than at any time in history.

Interactive conversations allow you to engage every customer who visits your web page in a personalized experience that reflects the values of both you and your business, enhancing your ability to convert visitors into customers while simultaneously guaranteeing that every customer experience will be consistently positive.

Social media tools remove almost every obstacle that formerly prevented you from engaging with exactly those customers who want and need your products the most, and at a fraction of the cost of traditional marketing. And highly efficient new tools – such as QR Codes and Mobile SMS – that make it even easier for businesses to connect with their customers are being created every day.

By carefully crafting your company's brand and your personal reputation, you can create a fun and lively experience that your customers will naturally want to be a part of. And by empowering your employees so that they have a stake in the success of your business, you can nurture your village so that it is a place where everybody wants to work.

An Exciting Time for Businesses!

This is an exciting time to be in business because the traditional walls that separate businesses from their customers – and that in the past separated businesses from their neighbors – are being torn down. Cross marketing gives you opportunities to build relationships with new partners that never existed before.

The new business paradigm means businesses no longer need to be soulless, dreary labor houses, but traveling parties where people genuinely enjoy each other's company and are devoted to the village's success.

All these wonderful tools – interactive conversations, social media, social comment sites, and the rest, can be used to create one ongoing online conversation, a village where businesses can maintain continual interaction with their customers, cross-marketing partners and local communities.

And the result is not only increased profits, better customer satisfaction, more referrals, lower operating expenses and better understanding of customer's desires, but more importantly a better and more successful business model that will continue to thrive deep into the 21st century and beyond.

About the Author

Tim Dini is a nationally recognized authority on marketing in the digital age; focusing on customer acquisition and retention.

Tim worked 32 years in the home service industry with hands-on expertise in the day-to-day operations of running a customer focused physical business. He has experienced both sides of business marketing; as a buyer and a creator of marketing services, giving him a unique perspective rarely found in the digital marketing industry.

Contact Information: **www.timdini.com**

References

"To Fully Enjoy YP, Please Upgrade to a Newer Browser." *YP.com*. N.p., n.d. Web. 04 Jan. 2016.

"Apple - IOS 6 - Use Your Voice to Do Even More with Siri." *Apple - IOS 6 - Use Your Voice to Do Even More with Siri*. N.p., n.d. Web. 04 Jan. 2016.

"Amazon.com: Online Shopping for Electronics, Apparel, Computers, Books, DVDs & More." *Amazon.com: Online Shopping for Electronics, Apparel, Computers, Books, DVDs & More*. N.p., n.d. Web. 04 Jan. 2016. <http://www.amazon.com/>.

"Trader Joe's." *Trader Joe's*. N.p., n.d. Web. 04 Jan. 2016. <http://traderjoes.com/stores/index.asp>.

"Welcome to Quaker Oats." *Welcome to Quaker Oats*. N.p., n.d. Web. 04 Jan. 2016. <http://www.quakeroats.com/home.aspx>.

"PepsiCo Home | PepsiCo.com." *RSS*. N.p., n.d. Web. 04 Jan. 2016. <http://www.pepsico.com/>.

"TiVo Premiere: Much More than a DVR - TiVo." *TiVo Premiere: Much More than a DVR - TiVo*. N.p., n.d. Web. 04 Jan. 2016. <http://www.tivo.com/>.

"NetFlix" *NetFlix: Watch TV Shows Online, Watch Movies Online* N.p., n.d. Web. 04 Jan. 2016

"Twitter" *Twitter* N.p., n.d. Web. 04 Jan. 2016. <http://twitter.com>.

"Groupon." *Groupon*. N.p., n.d. Web. 04 Jan. 2016. <http://www.groupon.com/>.

"Log In | Facebook." *Log In | Facebook*. N.p., n.d. Web. 04 Jan. 2016. <http://www.facebook.com/profile.php>.

"Google." *Google*. N.p., n.d. Web. 04 Jan. 2016. <https://plus.google.com/>.

"The Official Phil Spector Site." *The Official Phil Spector Site*. N.p., n.d. Web. 04 Jan. 2016. <http://www.philspector.com/>.

"Experience ABC Online." *ABC*. N.p., n.d. Web. 04 Jan. 2016. <http://abc.go.com/>.

"CBS." *TV Network Primetime, Daytime, Late Night and Classic Television Shows*. N.p., n.d. Web. 04 Jan. 2016. <http://www.cbs.com/>.